TRUE DECEIT FALSE LOVE

SETTING HEALTHY BOUNDARIES

after surviving Domestic Violence, Narcissistic Abuse,
Parental Alienation, Intergenerational Family Trauma
& Best Friend Betrayal

Dr. Marni Hill Foderaro

BALBOA.PRESS
A DIVISION OF HAY HOUSE

This book is a work of non-fiction. Unless otherwise noted, the author and the publisher make no explicit guarantees as to the accuracy of the information contained in this book and in some cases, names of people and places have been altered to protect their privacy.

Balboa Press books may be ordered through booksellers or by contacting:

Balboa Press
A Division of Hay House
1663 Liberty Drive
Bloomington, IN 47403
www.balboapress.com
844-682-1282

Because of the dynamic nature of the Internet, any web addresses or links contained in this book may have changed since publication and may no longer be valid. The views expressed in this work are solely those of the author and do not necessarily reflect the views of the publisher, and the publisher hereby disclaims any responsibility for them.

The author of this book does not dispense medical advice or prescribe the use of any technique as a form of treatment for physical, emotional, or medical problems without the advice of a physician, either directly or indirectly. The intent of the author is only to offer information of a general nature to help you in your quest for emotional and spiritual well-being. In the event you use any of the information in this book for yourself, which is your constitutional right, the author and the publisher assume no responsibility for your actions.

Any people depicted in stock imagery provided by Getty Images are models, and such images are being used for illustrative purposes only. Certain stock imagery © Getty Images.

ISBN: 979-8-7652-4604-7 (sc)
ISBN: 979-8-7652-4605-4 (e)

Library of Congress Control Number: 2023920866

Print information available on the last page.

WestBow Press rev. date: 02/02/2024

Everyone deserves the opportunity to be in positive relationships which are based on a foundation of honesty and mutual respect. There may come a time in our life when we realize that some of our relationships are not healthy, balanced or positive, and may even be toxic and/or psychologically damaging. When our lightbulb eventually goes on illuminating years of ignored Red Flags and our Inner Voice speaks to the gut-wrenching reality that we feel betrayed, used and Abused, causing us to think "No More; Enough is Enough," we need to stop and pay attention, and step back to really take a hard look at the company we keep. We need to learn about and practice Setting Healthy Boundaries.

"Daring to set boundaries is about having
the courage to love ourselves, even when
we risk disappointing others."
~Brene Brown

CONTENTS

"Boundaries are a sign of self-respect.
They're the cornerstone of healthy relationships."
~ Alyssa Nobriga

DISCLAIMER

Trigger Warning to proceed with caution! The information and examples in this **_TRUE DECEIT FALSE LOVE_** volume on Setting Healthy Boundaries provided in this book are on an "as is" basis and intended for informational, educational and entertainment purposes only, and should not be understood to constitute a medical, psychological or psychiatric diagnosis, healthcare recommendation or legal advice. The author's intent is to build awareness and provide examples to help the reader understand Healthy Boundaries and heal from the trauma of experiencing Domestic Violence, Narcissistic Abuse, Parental Alienation, Intergenerational Family Trauma and Best Friend Betrayal. The author and publisher make no representations or warranties of any kind with respect to the contents in this book and assume no responsibility for errors, inaccuracies, omissions or any other inconsistencies herein. Reading this book is at your own risk and you agree to take full responsibility for any resulting consequences. The information in this book is not a substitution for direct expert assistance and may be triggering. The motivation of the author is to provide information, assistance and support to others who may need to set Healthy Boundaries in their relationships. Please seek legal advice or professional help from a medical, psychological, psychiatric or healthcare specialist if necessary. This work is informational with depictions of some actual yet obscured examples, much like a memoir, in the life of the author as objectively truthfully as present recollections over time permits, without revealing any names or identifying characteristics. The author is not an expert or licensed provider on Domestic Violence, Narcissistic Abuse, Parental Alienation, Intergenerational Family Trauma or Best Friend Betrayal, and is not responsible for any resulting consequences, and the use of this book implies your acceptance of this disclaimer.

"Boundary Setting helps you prioritize your needs over other people's wants."
~ Lauren Kenson

DEDICATION

"You get what you tolerate."
~ Henry Cloud

**Setting Healthy Boundaries is necessary in our relationships
and essential to our own well-being and self-care.**

This 6th volume of my prominently endorsed, multi-book series
"TRUE DECEIT FALSE LOVE" is lovingly dedicated to all of the many
expert influencers, authors, podcasters, therapists, life coaches, teachers,
spiritual healers and just very wonderful people, including victims,
survivors and thrivers, who have devoted their time, talent and energy to
help so many of us understand ourselves and others as we work hard to set
Healthy Boundaries and learn about, heal from and triumph over Domestic
Violence, Narcissistic Abuse, Parental Alienation, Intergenerational Family
Trauma & Best Friend Betrayal.

You are appreciated, valued and loved.

PREFACE

A Heartfelt Note From The Author

You teach people how to treat you by what you allow,
what you stop and what you reinforce."
~ Tony Gaskins

When you eventually realize that you have been the Target of Domestic Violence, Narcissistic Abuse, Parental Alienation, Intergenerational Family Trauma and/or Best Friend Betrayal at the hands of a person or persons you cared for and trusted with unconditional love, in some cases unknowingly enduring this Intimate Partner Terrorism, Trauma Bond and Family Abuse for decades, your entire world is turned upside down. Learning to set and enforce Healthy Boundaries can play a key role in staying true to your values on your Healing Journey.

After the initial shock of realizing that you ignored years of glaring Red Flags as you were significantly betrayed and deceitfully manipulated, you muster up the courage to escape in the hopes that you can reclaim your life before it's too late. You acknowledge that there are huge repercussions to stepping back from or leaving your Abuser(s). Life as you knew it will never be the same. Your mind races as you now have to consider your basic safety and survival needs of food, shelter, money, transportation and employment. There are family ties for most, and we must contemplate the consequences and impact of our choices on others, especially our immediate family and children.

Some of us are forced to stay because we lack the inner strength or resources to escape, are afraid of or don't think we are capable of making such a drastic change or we have young children with our Abuser and instinctively must look out for our children's safety and well-being. Other Victims take time to carefully get their situations and assets in order so that they have a better chance at a more comfortable exit. Many of us just follow our gut instincts and knee-jerk reactions, using our best judgment and remove ourselves from the toxic situation and separate ourselves from the Abusive person or persons and environment at our earliest chance, leaving without a well-thought-out plan.

Abusers and Alienators are Predators and they don't usually let their Targeted Prey or Victims go easily or without a fight. The Abuser's need to keep up their False Public Persona by Smearing and Abusing their Victim can go on for years and even decades. Their malevolence is actually entertainment for them as they enjoy the power, control, chaos and confrontations. Most of these destructive individuals have traits of Mental Illness and if they would ever seek professional help or as a Cluster B Personality Disordered Covert Malignant Narcissist, Psychopath and/or Sociopath.

No two Abusers are alike as each person's behavior and personality falls on a spectrum of severity. Many of these Abusers want to discredit and destroy their Targets, especially when the truth of the Abuser's behaviors, deceit, lack of integrity and possibly even criminal behavior may be exposed. However, they all seem to feel that they are above the law and that society's rules don't apply to them; that's why they are so immoral, cutthroat and dishonest. They believe in their false perceived power of superiority. Somehow they all follow the same general playbook, so their extremely vindictive behaviors and responses to your setting Healthy Boundaries are often textbook predictable.

Significant harm is caused to innocent Victims as these scheming Abusers are known to methodically Gaslight their Targets for years. These Abusers mirror your positive traits and values because they are like empty vessels who lack empathy and morals, yet strive to fit into the mainstream to carry out their dirty and devious deeds. In the beginning of the relationship they engage in Mirroring and state that they value and care about all of the same things that you do. You are put on a pedestal as the Love Bombing and Future Faking sucks you into the illusion that you have finally met your soulmate. You pinch yourself because the relationship seems too good to be true. You don't see the obvious Bait-and Hook strategy. You may believe that you are living in a fairytale, and you eventually and comfortably settle into living the coveted "American Dream."

Over time, however, you begin to feel confused and experience bouts of Cognitive Dissonance as the Abuser acts one way around others, flaunting their created Public Persona to maintain their False Image behind a mask, and another way with you behind closed doors. You may begin to doubt yourself, your discernment or your abilities. Your physical health suffers and you may develop autoimmune diseases because slowly, without you knowing it, your body and mind have been in "fight or flight" survival mode. Eventually your identity and perspectives are so fundamentally distorted due to the inflicted Trauma that you lose your previously solid confidence and find yourself dependent on your Abuser as he/she now has the authority over the purse strings and everything in your environment, including who you can see, what you can do and where and when you can go. Your Abuser's controlling actions do not match his/her words. You are trapped and stifled with little or no freedom, but you accept your circumstances because these constraints are presented under the cloak of care and concern for your well-being. Besides, you are busy focusing on your job, home and family, honoring the vows you made under God and have invested so much time and commitment to this relationship that you plug along thinking and trusting that things will get better as you hope for the best.

These calculating Perpetrators begin to accuse you and others of their own wrongdoings and unethical or illegal activities. Behind your back, they viciously Smear your name to everyone and anyone in your circle with outlandish lies and believable half-truths. They gain support and sympathy by playing the Victim to people who end up being Flying Monkeys, doing the bidding and spying for the Abuser. These Abusers are also Alienators who Brainwash your children, family, friends, neighbors, coworkers and countless others in cult-like fashion to believe that you are a bad or sick person who should be avoided and feared. They accuse their Targets of cheating, stealing and lying, when the reality is that they are the ones cheating, stealing and lying. These ruthless bullies lack empathy and engage in Projection which is done with such careful planning and malevolent intent, setting the stage for when the relationship will eventually dissolve, either through a planned or unexpected Discard or your untimely death. In addition to their numerous extramarital escapades, these Secret Agent men and women keep in contact with old flames and are always on the prowl to line up replacement relationships in their Harem Closet in the event that they choose to Discard you as their main source of supply, or worse yet for the Abuser, you become wise to their games and choose to leave them to cautiously carry out your escape.

It's usually not until after you separate from the Abuser that you realize that you are left with no support system or money; your lifelong friends and long-term neighbors become Flying Monkeys for the Abuser and give you the cold shoulder, wanting nothing to do with you anymore. It's shocking because you thought that these close relationships were strong and you took for granted that they would always be there for you. In stealth fashion, the Abusers utilize the Divide and Conquer method and focus their Campaign of Denigration on those closest to us, so even your relationship with your family members and best friends surprisingly change as well. These revengeful and vindictive Perpetrators fear being exposed and their False Public Persona and malevolent intentions and actions revealed to the masses who they've fooled for years. Legal justice does not usually seem to prevail for the Targeted Victims as the family court system is often part of the problem, but if you escape and do the research, inner reflection and Shadow Work, you have a great chance of moving forward, starting over with rebuilding your life and eventually finding peace, harmony and true love.

Abusers are also obsessed with stealing and manipulating money and are often fiscally irresponsible as they create chaotic financial calculations, scenarios and debts. Most Victims find that their cash and assets have been suddenly depleted and their house goes into foreclosure even when for years they were told and believed that the family home was paid off. The Victim learns that all of the joint charge cards are maxed out and new credit cards were fraudulently opened up with their forged name and social security number. These Abusers illegally engage in Identity Theft and even steal their own kids' money from their bank accounts, empty their college funds, cash in their savings bonds and take out credit cards in their children's names without them ever knowing. It's not until years later that you may find out that the Abusers's urgent need for large sums of cash is to fund their double or triple life of pornography, gambling and/or substance abuse addictions, private investments, hidden assets or even to support another family or love-children they never disclosed to you; many adult children are shocked to later find out that they have half-siblings that were secretly kept from them. Many of these Adult Children never find out the truth and stay aligned with their lying, Abusing, Alienating Parent their entire life.

A very common coping mechanism for the Victims who are courageous enough to escape the Abusive Relationship is to try to make sense of how and why such bad things can happen to such good people. You, as the honest Empath who was betrayed, are compelled to play the role of detective as you begin to seek information and confirmation though your own investigations using computer searches, literature research, books, blogs, YouTube videos, podcasts and therapeutic counseling. You try to get answers to your many questions in an attempt to put a name to your feelings and experiences. You quickly find that you are not alone and that there is a huge support network out there of professionals and everyday people who have experienced Domestic Violence, Narcissistic Abuse, Parental Alienation and Intergenerational Family Trauma, and often, as part of their own healing process, are driven to provide awareness, resources and support to others.

Recovering from the extreme Complex Trauma and stress of this type of Abuse is a process and takes a great deal of time. Victims are forced to navigate through significant shock and loss as they experience each of the stages of grief. You may have been able to move on or move far away to reclaim your life and start over, but you continue to be haunted by your experiences and dashed hopes for your future. Most of us have to deal with breaking Trauma Bonds and our Abuser's continued emotional, physical or legal stalking and harassment for years, in extreme cases, even decades. Abusers enjoy taking you back to court. They are the ones left with a great deal of money to misuse the justice system in frivolous lawsuits against you. They love the feeling of being dominant over their Victim as they deplete your time, energy, money and resources. You may feel alone and lonely as your support system has vanished, although in time, this period of Isolation can prove to be helpful as you quietly regain your independence and inner strength.

During your recovery efforts of self-healing and self-love and to understand your role in this unfortunate situation, it is helpful to reflect on and examine your family of origin dynamics and acknowledge your own childhood Traumas, Abandonment issues, Core Wounds and probable Intergenerational Abuse that most likely contributed to your naivety and unmet emotional needs which eventually lead you to choosing toxic, controlling and Abusive partnerships. This history may have also contributed to you trusting too much too soon, being an over-giver or having weak boundaries, making you the perfect Target for your Abuser. It is so very necessary to value yourself enough to set and enforce Healthy Boundaries with everyone in your circle.

You probably came across this book as a result of your quest for knowledge on this topic. Well, I'm glad you did and hopefully the timing was synchronistic with where you are at in your inquiry and healing journey. This 6th volume *TRUE DECEIT FALSE LOVE Setting Healthy Boundaries after surviving Domestic Violence, Narcissistic Abuse,*

Parental Alienation, Intergenerational Family Trauma & Best Friend Betrayal, will hopefully provide you with much needed information and validation. Just reading through the examples in this book will give you some awareness to setting limits and understanding the relationship traumas associated with much of what you may have experienced. There are numerous and varied reasons when it comes to why someone would need to set Healthy Boundaries. Doing your own research while you are simultaneously connecting the dots to your own experiences can be very therapeutic and an integral part of the healing process and your personal growth.

In closing, I would like to offer hope and encouragement to all of the men, women, children and families who find themselves navigating Domestic Violence, Narcissistic Abuse, Parental Alienation, Intergenerational Family Trauma and Best Friend Betrayal. Know that you are a beautiful, loving soul who should be treated with kindness and respect. You are not crazy. You didn't do anything to deserve the malicious treatment you previously received or are currently receiving at the hands of your Abusing spouse, friend, acquaintance, neighbor, colleague, boss, coach, therapist, parent, adult child and/or extended family member and their aligned cohorts. Don't be hard on yourself that it took you so long to finally see things for what they really are; Abusers are very calculating and skilled Master-Manipulators and put great efforts into hiding their covert venomous, vindictive and vile deceit behind their Fraudulent Mask. Remember, nobody is perfect and we are all here to grow as individuals as we learn life's lessons. You know the truth and the facts of what you've been through.

Try to look objectively at what has happened to you so you can unlearn negative patterns and steer away from unhealthy tendencies as you become more vigilant in recognizing Abusive people and situations, while understanding yourself more. The family, friends, neighbors, coworkers and acquaintances that you lose because you set Healthy Boundaries or no longer resonate with them, their behavior or values make room for new relationships with like-minded people of integrity. Watch out for the Hoovers; Abusers often return to suck you back in. Be willing to change and get out of your comfort zone. Reflect on the values that are meaningful to you and stay true to them. Honor who you are. Acknowledge your feelings. Manage the Triggers. Choose to respond, not react, to life's challenges. Embrace your authenticity as you gather up your strength to strive for independence and personal growth while you get back on your feet. You have what it takes to get through this. Knowledge is power. Setting Healthy Boundaries will help you reclaim your life.

Understanding yourself, as well as learning the dynamics of toxic individuals who engage in Domestic Violence, Narcissistic Abuse, Parental Alienation, Intergenerational Family Trauma and/ or Best Friend Betrayal can be very enlightening and help empower you to move towards peace and Self-Actualization. You need to take responsibility for your role, foundational patterns and Trauma Bonds which made you a perfect Target for Abuse. You must change, as you cannot and should not ever go back to how things were. You are stronger than you know. Your Survivor Voice matters.

You have the power within you to set and enforce Healthy Boundaries.

Turn your negative experiences into positive opportunities to evolve into the genuine person that you were meant to be. Don't be surprised if you experience some type of Spiritual Awakening and are now more in tune with the universe's signs and synchronicities. Have faith. This may be a good time to reconnect, embrace and trust in a Higher Source.

You never know, God could even come to your garage sale!

My sincere hope is that this book on Setting Healthy Boundaries, the 6th volume of my prominently endorsed, multi-book series **TRUE DECEIT FALSE LOVE,** will provide you with much needed information and validation. Stay strong as you take back your power to live a beautifuland fulfilling life. You deserve more and the best is yet to come. Truth eventually prevails.

I wish you compassion, goodness and peace on your Healing Journey. Much love and light to you.

Many Blessings Always,
Marni

"Setting boundaries or calling out toxic behavior isn't hateful, it's sacred and it should be taught in every Spiritual practice."
~Shahida Arabi

FOREWORD

BY TRACY A. MALONE

Dr. Marni Hill Foderaro and I have connected through our shared experiences and the bond of becoming "surTHRIVERS" after experiencing Narcissistic Abuse. When a Targeted Victim has been in an Abusive relationship, several factors can make them more vulnerable and Trauma-Bonded. These may include qualities such as being a compassionate Empath, having codependent tendencies, over-giving and/or being a people-pleaser. However, what Abusers specifically target is someone with weak boundary-setting skills.

After years of attempting to establish Healthy Boundaries with others that were consistently disregarded, I reached a point where I almost considered giving up trying to stand up for myself by speaking up and staying true to my values. The notion crossed my mind that I might not be skilled at setting Healthy Boundaries. It was only through my honest, insightful conversations and inspiring friendship with Marni that I began to recognize numerous people in my life, including immediate family members, with whom my boundaries had never proven effective. This realization prompted me to research and do a deep-dive to understand the importance of strengthening my boundaries with everyone, and to conclude that those who didn't respect my boundaries didn't have a place in my life. As painful and uncomfortable as it was, it became necessary for me to let go of these toxic, unhealthy and unbalanced relationships.

As a global Narcissistic Abuse Coach, my mission is to empower Survivors to thrive and become "surTHRIVERS" who assert their boundaries and prevent being taken advantage of in their future relationships. In addition to my in-person and online coaching, I am also a best-selling author, experienced teacher, regular podcaster and sought-after international speaker who provides workshops, classes, healing journals and numerous resources, all of which can be found on my website www.NarcissistAbuseSupport.com.

In this book, Marni provides real-life examples and stories that illustrate situations where individuals may find it necessary to establish, set and enforce Healthy Boundaries. Whether you're dealing with a romantic partner, family members, friends or coworkers, Dr. Marni Hill Foderaro offers practical advice to assist you in your awareness as you learn to finally value yourself and your worth, and determine what you will and will no longer tolerate in relationships.

I believe that Dr. Marni Hill Foderaro's work in this book on Setting Healthy Boundaries, as in all of her books in her prominently-endorsed and award-winning book series "TRUE DECEIT FALSE LOVE," is essential for shedding light on situations that may require improved boundary-setting skills.

~Tracy A. Malone
Author, Teacher, Coach, surTHRIVER and Founder of
NarcissistAbuseSupport.com, a global resource for Survivors

"Most say settng boundaries with a Narcissist rarely works. I suggest that the act of trying to set a boundary (despite its most likely negative response and results) is far better than never trying at all. For when you surrender and stop trying to set boundaries, Abusers get their way, and they win. Never stop fighting to be valued as you should be."
-Tracy A. Malone

AUTHOR BIOGRAPHY

www.GodCameToMyGarageSale.com

Dr. Marni Hill Foderaro is a multi-award-winning and celebrated author, speaker and educator. She earned her doctorate in education from Northern Illinois University and completed postdoctoral studies at Harvard during a very successful and rewarding 35-year career as a high school special education teacher, with 12 years as a university graduate school adjunct professor. Marni's life was forever changed after experiencing numerous trauma-induced STEs-Spiritually Transformative Encounters. Marni's 2022 Hollywood Book Fest runner-up, 2020 Best Books finalist Award Winning and 5-Star Reader's Favorite Spiritual fiction, inspired by true events, *"GOD CAME TO MY GARAGE SALE"* is prominently endorsed by James Redfield, best selling author of *"The Celestine Prophecy"* series of books, and other notables in the Spiritual community, including founding directors of IANDS (International Association for Near Death Studies). Marni's latest prominently endorsed multi-book series entitled: *"TRUE DECEIT FALSE LOVE"* creatively addresses and provides tools and resources for understanding and healing from Domestic Violence, Narcissistic Abuse, Parental Alienation and Intergenerational Family Trauma. Marni is a lover of animals, nature, music and world travel who handles life's challenges with love and compassion. She values honesty, integrity, equality and goodness and prays for peace on earth. Marni was born in the South, raised her children in the Midwest and lives in the Caribbean. In addition to her TV/podcast interviews, speaking engagements and various writing endeavors on embracing Spirituality after surviving Domestic Violence, Narcissistic Abuse, Parental Alienation and Intergenerational Family Trauma, Marni is a contributing author to numerous anthology books, including: *"The Last Breath," "The Evolution of Echo," "We're All In This Together: Embrace One Another," "Passing The Pearls," "Write & Publish Your Book," "The Ulti-MUTT Book for Dog Lovers"* and *"bLU Talks Presents"* *(Business, Life and the Universe.)* In 2022 Dr. Marni Hill Foderaro was inducted into the Bestselling Authors International (BAI) Organization.

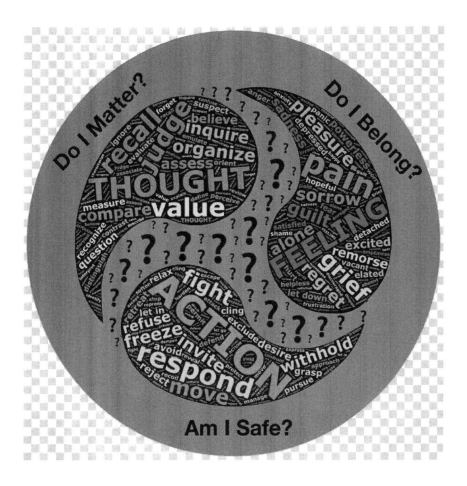

"*The more you value yourself, the healthier your boundaries are.*"
~ *Lorraine Nilon*

SETTING HEALTHY BOUNDARIES

"The purpose of setting boundaries is to protect and take care
of ourselves. We need to be able to tell other people when
they are acting in ways that are not acceptable to us."
~ Melody Beattie

Everyone deserves the opportunity to be in positive relationships based on a foundation of honesty and mutual respect. There may come a time in our life when we realize that some of our relationships are not healthy, balanced or positive, and may even be toxic and/or psychologically damaging. When our lightbulb eventually goes on illuminating years of ignored Red Flags and our Inner Voice speaks to the gut-wrenching reality that we feel betrayed, used and Abused, causing us to think "No More; Enough is Enough," we need to stop and pay attention, and step back to really take a hard look at the company we keep. We need to learn about and practice Setting Healthy Boundaries.

We may have experienced, and may also be currently experiencing, physical, emotional, sexual and/or financial violations done to us by spouses, partners, coworkers, friends and/or family members where we feel taken advantage of, hurt, discounted and disrespected. These people may not be aware that their actions are oppressive and cause us great discomfort. Another, more painful reality that we may come to find out, is that their manipulative behavior may be intentional, rooted in their misguided need for power and coercive control and has malevolent and narcissistic underpinnings.

After the shock of finally acknowledging the betrayal and Abuse from someone we thought loved and cared for us the same way we loved and cared for them, we should ideally take the time to strategize how to address this revelation. Often times we react in knee-jerk fashion, when the more sensible action is to think through the situation, analyze the history of the relationship dynamic, including our role, and systematically plot out our response leading to a carefully-planned resolution. Do we try to use reason and communicate authentically, do we confront and call them out or do we just go "No Contact," plan our escape and quietly release these people from our life?

We need to value our own worth and honor ourselves, which means we may need to put up and set Healthy Boundaries, even if it is with people we've known our entire life and love dearly, including close friends and family. Healthy Boundaries are limits that we can set to prevent other people from overstepping their bounds and engaging in a way that makes us feel uncomfortable, hurt or taken advantage of. Boundaries are the ability to know what is positive or right for us and what is negative or wrong for us. We've been conditioned, many of us our entire lives, to suppress our own thoughts when it comes to Cognitive Dissonance and feeling dismissed or devalued in our relationships. So many of us empathetic souls have an ingrained need to people-please and over-give, which is a result of years of Gaslighting, self-doubt, anxiety and just wanting to be loved.

I have personally found that letting go and going No Contact seems to be the most effective and appropriate decision for me when it comes to putting up Healthy Boundaries and choosing to value myself over the toxic, Abusive and unhealthy people in my life. I would rather take all of the pain at once and let go, rather than experience years of a drawn out process that most likely wouldn't even result in a more positive outcome. Even if these decisions to remove certain people from our day-to-day are painful and filled with a wide array of conflicting emotions, including sadness, shock, guilt, anger, and shame, walking away from negativity and/or Abuse after realizing who you are dealing with can provide an initial respite to the pressing angst and put a stop to experiencing their Abuse, at least temporarily. It's not easy to put up and enforce Healthy Boundaries, especially when it's something we have never done before. We need to break the familiar pattern and conditioning of caring more about others than we care about ourselves.

If we finally begin to notice that some of our relationships are not based on mutual respect, or even if we have suspected this for some time and ignored years of glaring Red Flags or disregarded our spot-on Gut Intuition that someone in our life doesn't seem to truly care about us, is interested in us, value our feelings or respect our differing views on issues, and if our thoughts or what's important to us, and our interactions with them leaves us with feelings of hurt, resentfulness or being taken advantage of, then we need to take a closer look as to whether staying in these relationships is positive or negative for our overall mental health and happiness. We may need to set Healthy Boundaries.

Because we are empathetic, compassionate, caring, honest and open individuals, a reasonable response and action step to naturally address these concerns would be for us to initiate a candid conversation with our friend or family member, to honestly discuss our feelings about what we see as the betrayal in the unequal relationship dynamic. We may share what hurts us or what makes us uncomfortable, expecting mutual respect, in the hopes that there will be understanding, resulting in a change to rectify our concerns. I caution you, however, when it comes to choosing this reasonable response. This opens up the Abuser's ability to manipulate the situation by strategically placating you with their Word Salad or Love Bombing. I have learned firsthand that you cannot use logic and reason with unreasonable or narcissistic people. I encourage you to pay more attention to their actions rather than to their words. People's behavior can speak volumes.

The reaction of our friend or family member to us putting up Healthy Boundaries is also an indication of whether we are in a healthy relationship or whether we are in a toxic or psychologically Abusive relationship. Their response really tells us everything we need to know. Abusive others don't like it when we finally have the courage to stand up for ourselves and set a Healthy Boundary. Many will use Projection and turn the situation around and will use Blame Shifting to start accusing us for what they are actually doing. They may ramp up their Gaslighting of us to try and get us to question our reality and our decision to stand up for ourselves. They may react with anger, even Narcissistic Rage. They may give us the Silent Treatment or Grey Rock us. They most likely will begin a devastating Smear Campaign, trashing our good character with a False Narrative of outright lies and believable half-truths, to gather up Flying Monkey support from those in our circle (such as friends, family, neighbors, coworkers, even our own children). Some will apologize, promise to change or Love Bomb us to get us to go back to how things were; we may fall for these attempts and on a rare occasion they may be sincere, however, these reactions most likely are a calculated effort to temporarily get us back to where they want us, under their domineering power and Coercive Control. They turn the tables on us and although they are the ones mistreating us, they will pull out the Victim Card to gain the sympathy of those around them. The Abuse Cycle can then be repeated.

On a more positive note, if someone truly values us, their empathetic and sincere response to our honestly expressing our feelings will be loving and reassuring. Healthy people want to respect us and realize that Boundaries are used to keep people IN our life, which allows them to stay in our circle. This also gives others the opportunity to let us know that they do sincerely care about our feelings and will gladly make changes to improve the relationship.

On the negative side, it is hard to learn and painful to come to terms with the reality that there are people in our life who we love and care for, many who have been in our life for years and years, who do not truly value our feelings or concerns and show that by their negative response to our desire to communicate our feelings about some aspect of the relationship dynamic. Our need to put up Healthy Boundaries may be met with opposition or a reaction that we were not expecting. A negative reaction may look like ignoring or dismissing our concerns, making the situation all about them, turning on us by blaming us, making us feel guilty for our feelings, or saying that we are too sensitive, that we have misinterpreted their actions or that we really didn't hear what we heard or saw what we saw or feel what we felt. We may be deeply Trauma-Bonded with these friends or family members, who have diminished our self-worth and confidence when we choose to speak up for ourselves. We've allowed these ingrained patterns to continue and increase.

Abusive people may be undiagnosed Covert Malignant Narcissists who are controlling, manipulative and will often resort to Gaslighting and Projection. They love confrontation and seem to thrive on conflict or our unhappiness and self-doubt. These people will often engage in a Smear Campaign, where they will turn others against us with a False Narrative created with outright lies and believable half-truths. It can be shocking to lose people in our life because of the back-stabbing efforts of someone we were previously close to, just because we decided to put up a Healthy Boundary. As painful as this is, it's better to know the type of person we are dealing with. It is better to shrink our circle, rather than keep things the way they were. It's better to live with quality relationships, rather than quantity. We really learn who has our back and truly cares for us, and who doesn't. Toxic and/or psychologically Abusive people do not truly love us or respect us.

We set Healthy Boundaries to honor ourselves. The more we set Healthy Boundaries with romantic relationships, friends, coworkers, neighbors and family members, the more we learn about ourselves and the people in our lives. Putting up Healthy Boundaries is not about us being mean or selfish or used by us as a form of punishment in a relationship; we may still truly love these people. But, we must love ourselves more and believe we deserve to be treated well. Putting up Healthy Boundaries is a step towards us being self- aware of the relationship dynamics we are in. As we get stronger and more secure and confident in who we are, we can overcome and heal our relationship challenges. This can positively impact future relationships because we learn about what behaviors we will and will not tolerate, and we can then decide who we let in or keep in our lives.

For us to put up Healthy Boundaries, we must communicate what we expect and need in our relationships, including what we will or will not allow or tolerate. We need to pay attention to Red Flags and listen to our Gut Intuition for the signs that indicate that things are not positive, healthy or balanced. If something doesn't feel right, it probably isn't good for us. If someone's actions gives us negative thoughts or a feeling of being uncomfortable, then we need to pay attention. At all times we must protect our safety, both physically and emotionally. We cannot control the feelings, actions or reactions of others; we can only control ourselves and how we respond. We may need to reevaluate our relationships and change the level of contact with these individuals. With some, even though they will disagree and turn on us, going No Contact may be the only productive choice for our own peace and well-being.

For me, when I finally valued myself enough to exercise the courage to put up Healthy Boundaries with certain friends and family members and address the relational adversity and the negative feelings I felt after interacting with them or their efforts to instill guilt and shame or silence me back into the pattern of obedience and submission, I found the strength, courage and clarity to give myself permission to get out of these relationships, even though I may truly love the ones that I believe are hurting me.

We need to stay true to our own values. My personal values include honesty, love, compassion and goodness. It is then that we move closer to living a more self-actualized life with more integrity as our Authentic

Self. We must do the Deep Dive into our own healing to understand what it is about us that makes us a Target for being treated poorly. We must acknowledge our feelings and accept that we are where we are at this given point in time. We must research and learn the lessons through deep Inner Reflection or getting therapeutic help to heal from our negative experiences and understand the patterns of our Intergenerational Family Traumas. If we don't look within and take responsibility by doing the Inner Shadow Work, then we are not moving forward on our path to understanding ourselves and others. Ignoring this integral step also enables the continuation of the bad behavior of others by indirectly giving them permission to keep going along as things were, which allows the acceptance of our negative feelings.

The resulting consequences to us setting Healthy Boundaries with close friends and family may be shockingly unexpected and quite painful, but we must stay strong in our decision to walk away and to honor ourselves. We must accept the reactions and outcomes, whether the resulting response is positive or negative. I've experienced this firsthand and know how devastating some people's reactions can be to your standing up for yourself, even if it is over some issue that is very minor. So often, we fear negative outcomes if we openly communicate our thoughts with a close friend or family member, especially if our perspective differs from theirs. This fear leads to us remaining silent and not addressing the issues to move forward. If we are expressing that their actions or words make us feel less than, then there is a good chance they may react by going on the defensive. It is a natural response to fear rejection and results in us not wanting to "rock the boat." Sometimes it seems easier to continue the same old familiar patterns, ignore the situation and not communicate or confront, just to keep the Status Quo.

Setting Healthy Boundaries with close friends or family can come across to them as challenging, where they can become extremely defensive. They may react in ways we don't expect. It seems that this discord can bring out the worst in some people where they really show us their True Colors. We may even begin to see their Abuse, Narcissism or rigid Toxicity. We may finally be at a point in our own awareness that we recognize that their reaction is extreme, and we no longer feel comfortable in going along just to get along. This resulting interaction may cause us to reflect back on many times over the years where this was the case, but we diminished ourselves and our stance so we didn't upset the apple cart. In severe cases, these friends or family members may even ramp up their Abuse of us, even though we initially never looked at our interactions with them as Abusive. There are a few instances where I've experienced setting Healthy Boundaries which resulted in a complete change in the close relationship dynamic, both positive and negative. I'll provide some examples of setting Healthy Boundaries in romantic relationships, with friends, with coworkers and with family members that ended up to be huge life lessons for me on my growth and healing journey. We might lose them altogether.

When we muster up the courage to set Healthy Boundaries and we put in the conscientious effort to enforce them as we stay true to our values and worth, then our lives will be eventually be transformed in so many positive ways. We will break the unhealthy patterns that we have allowed and even encouraged to repeat in our lives. Change is up to us. We can't continue the same behavior and expect different results. This can be a crossroads turning point that will have many advantages to your emotional, physical, spiritual health and well-being. Your stress levels will be reduced because others who have previously taken advantage of your kindness, generosity and good nature will realize there are limits. If these are people who are meant to stay in your life, they will take the cue to respect you more because you are finally respecting yourself. You most likely will be more aware of and sensitive to others' boundaries as well. You'll be able to step back from unhealthy or time-consuming activities that directly or indirectly drain your energy and leave you with emotional discontent or baggage. It is time to value yourself. Setting Healthy Boundaries is a gift to yourself that keeps giving. You are worth it.

HEALTHY BOUNDARIES IN ROMANTIC RELATIONSHIPS

"Evaluating the benefits and drawbacks of any relationship is your responsibility. You do not have to to passively accept what is brought to you. You can choose."
~Deborah Day

When most of us hear people talking about the term "Healthy Boundaries" we usually think of setting some limits within romantic relationships, such as dating or marriage. In a dating scenario, when you are first starting to get to know someone and open up, this can be an opportune time to set initial limits in the relationship. These limits are set to prevent our date or prospective suitor from overstepping their bounds or engaging in a way that causes us to be uncomfortable. Taking the time to set Healthy Boundaries can be overlooked in the beginning of a relationship because we are often filled with excitement, anticipation and adrenaline and want to just go with our natural attraction and urges to get emotionally and/or physically close while we are initially getting to know someone. Boundaries can and do benefit both people in the relationship because they allow each person to preserve their own values of integrity. People move in relationships at their own pace, and that should be respected.

You may find that your dating partner is wanting to move faster in the relationship than you want to. If the pace is moving faster than your comfort level, you need to be able to effectively communicate that and know when to say "NO." If your date does not respect that and violates your wishes, then you have every right to reconsider whether or not you want to continue in this relationship. They could be testing you early on to see if you really mean what you say. If you begin to have feelings of anger, frustration or resentment as a result of even a minor violation of your boundaries, that should be a big sign, a big Red Flag, to end what was just begun. "Nip it in the bud." You might actually be the one who initiates a physical connection before really knowing who you are dealing with and what their personality or intentions are. Be careful that you don't contribute to reversing the order in the natural progression of relationships. In extreme cases, you must be very mindful when it comes to your safety in a dating situation, as some interactions unfortunately result in terrible outcomes, such as Date Rape or even murder.

Before you really get to know someone, make sure you meet in a public place, be careful about what personal details you share and be mindful of the substances you put in your body that may alter your judgment. It is better to be safe than sorry. Hopefully, with setting Healthy Boundaries, your dating experiences will be safe and positive. If they are not, realize that there are more respectful fish in the sea. Being able to clearly and effectively put up and enforce Healthy Boundaries is really laying a positive, open foundation in dating.

Many of us learn about Healthy Boundaries within our families, marriages or long-term relationships AFTER we have experienced and escaped Domestic Discord such as Narcissistic Abuse or Intimate Partner Violence. When we make a relationship commitment to another person, there is always some give and take. At least early on, our spouse or partner may be sensitive to our wants and needs, as well as what makes us happy, what makes us uncomfortable or what we will not tolerate. Over time, however, the Boundary Lines can get a bit blurred. Some of these Boundaries may revolve around our time, our home, our belongings, our emotional space, our parenting styles, our responsibilities (chores-the division of labor) and even our wants and needs regarding sexual intimacy. When we are in a committed relationship, we typically expect to grow together as a couple, so that boundaries are understood. Because of this, we often make assumptions that our partner is on the same page and so we don't bother to make it a priority to communicate our needs and limitations openly and honestly.

We may actually be partially at fault and contribute to our boundaries being violated by not speaking up and allowing overstepping to happen or continue. This can lead to a build up of resentment, which can negatively impact the relationship. Our partner can have many moments where they act loving and well-intentioned mixed with the negative, however, as many of us have learned the hard way, our partner may not truly care or have our best interests at heart, and may have a Double Life of Infidelity, deceit and/or fraud. Sometimes their true character may take years to come into your awareness, and often the Abuse is ramped up when they know that you know about their true character or after you separate or divorce. I experienced this firsthand. Our voices matter, so by objectively sharing the facts of our personal experiences, we can open up the conversation to enlighten others who may be enduring similar experiences, so that possibly we can prevent them from heartache and losses, as we embark on our own healing journey.

We also may be a sought-after Target by an Abuser. Covert Malignant Narcissistic Predators in search of their next Prey or Victim look for strong, independent, successful, beautiful and empathetic people of integrity who have experienced previous traumas and losses and have weak boundaries, so they can play the "Knight in Shining Armor" and swoop them off their feet with their Love Bombing, Mirroring and Future Faking. The reality is that this pursuit is a challenge and competitive game for Domestic Abusers to use their need for control and manipulation and see how much you will tolerate as they dim your light and have you doubt yourself and diminish your own self-worth.

In my case, I realize now that my foundational upbringing contributed to my being a Target for an Abuser. I initially was a product of a broken and dysfunctional home where the children were eventually used as pawns in my parents' war with each other during their extremely contentious divorce. At very young ages, we, the children, were even put on the stand in the courthouse! Of course, I have always chosen to hold onto the many positive takeaways from my childhood, but the years of erratic Intermittent Reinforcement led to Cognitive Dissonance and Trauma Bonding. I had no idea back then that I was neglected which resulted in my adult abandonment issues, which further led to my being a people-pleaser and over-giver. I knew our upbringing focused on survival and was much different than those of my neighborhood friends who had curfews and regular family dinner hours, while we were left on our own a great deal of the time to fend for ourselves. The cupboards were often empty and I remember going hungry a lot, embarrassing myself and causing concern by my friends' mothers at slumber parties when I would proceed to eat an entire box (or two or three) of cereal as if it were my last meal.

In my family, there was a great deal of sibling rivalry, which was allowed to continue without healthy parental intervention. Now I understand the Isolation tactics, Alienation and Divide and Conquer strategies an Abusive Parent will use to separate siblings from one another. My own children have been Isolated and Estranged from each other for years by their other parent, the Alienator, who keeps them separated and purposely discourages them from communicating or having a relationship with each other, I believe, so he can keep up his lies and False Narrative and the kids don't compare notes so he can keep his many secrets, Abuse and unethical wrongdoings safe from being exposed.

Growing up as I did, I never viewed myself as a Victim and always looked at myself as a fearless, strong-willed, independent Survivor, who was driven to leave home at an early age to become successful on my own. I knew of my father's alcoholism and numerous affairs and my mother's debilitating "mental illness." However, I know now and I believe after my own ordeal and my extensive research on Domestic Violence, that my mom was a Victim of severe Narcissistic Abuse and extreme Gaslighting, and back in those days, there was not support for Emotionally Abused wives, especially when their husbands held such admired, upstanding positions in the community. My father did what many Abusers do; he convinced my mom that she was unstable and unworthy, convinced others that she was crazy with a well-thought-out and damaging Smear Campaign and had her involuntarily committed to numerous psych wards over many years where she was permanently damaged with shock treatments and psychotic/psychotropic medications.

Her three suicide attempts as a young mother may be explained now by Postpartum Depression, but more likely resulted from the Intimate Partner Violence of years of ongoing Gaslighting and Narcissistic Abuse. All of this fed into the False Public Persona and resulting attention with family and community support that my Blame-Shifting dad was an innocent Victim deserving of others' sympathy, a narrative that he continues to stand by even into his 90's. My late mother used to tell me that I was God's favorite pupil because I always had to learn life lessons the hard way. She sure was right.

Additionally, in my college years, I experienced a few romantic relationships which ended abruptly, leaving me shocked, hurt and confused. I was always seeking a stable partnership, but looking back I may have come across as needy and desperate for love. When my now ex-husband met me, I had just been severely rejected from my college, live-in boyfriend who announced to me that he was in love with a girl I knew from my childhood who I introduced him to. He broke up with me a week before our enormous and elaborate wedding. Again I was shocked into yet another survival-mode situation. The hurt and betrayal seemed to be a familiar pattern to the ending of my romantic relationships. Looking back at this devastating break-up, I realized that it took a great deal of strength and courage for my then-fiancé to stay true to what he really wanted in a spouse and break up when he did, especially since there was pressure all around to follow through, and especially after all of the many bridal showers and all of my money and a huge amount of his parents' money was spent on the wedding and expensive reception. It was shortly after this rejection that I jumped into a long-term relationship with the person who I would eventually marry, and stay married to for 27 years.

I ignored every single Red Flag that there was in the relationship with my future spouse, but I was young and in love, as well as vulnerable and traumatized. I didn't know about Love Bombing, Future Faking, Hoovering and signs to watch out for that you are dealing with a Narcissist, Sociopath and/or Psychopath. I wish I knew then what I know now, but then I wouldn't have experienced the journey that I now believe was part of my life plan. Abusers seem to casually and accidentally confess to their unethical actions in a matter-of-fact way, so that the seriousness of what they've done goes unnoticed. The Target, though, has to also be in a state of Denial to overlook such blatant warnings. It's a Perfect Storm. At one point after three years of dating when we were getting close to marriage, my boyfriend (and later husband) informed me that his old girlfriend of eight years from out of state was living with him temporarily. My gut reaction was to break up immediately and move on, which I did. However, in his classic Hoover several months later, I was convinced that he loved only me and that we should be together forever. I later learned that he was involved with her a decade prior and they had continued a long-distance relationship where he was promising her the world. After divorcing, I learned that their relationship continued in one form or another over the three decades we were man and wife. Narcissists like to keep the doors open in their past relationships for when they need a Harem reconnect. That's why they return to their old flames, even while they are always in hot pursuit of fresh New Supply. Some Secret Agent Men in these situations end up having a "Love Child" who they use their "primary family's" finances to support and who may remain hidden for a lifetime. There have been numerous accounts of Adult Children eventually finding out that they have half-siblings they never knew about.

I was living the "American Dream," raising our two beautiful children, working in a fulfilling career as a high school special education teacher and university graduate school adjunct professor, residing in a gorgeous suburban home (complete with the quintessential white picket fence), studying for an advanced degree, pursuing my hobbies and interests, volunteering for worthwhile causes and enjoying a "fairytale life." I was on top of the world.

Sympathetically conscientious of others, I was always generous to those around me. A deep sense of compassion was woven into the fabric of my empathetic being. As a person of integrity who believes in honesty, commitments, perseverance and good will, I thought that everyone I was close to had those same intrinsic moral values. I naively thought that the people in my circle, my family, friends and especially my husband, were honest and respectful of me. I never thought I had to worry about Healthy Boundaries in my intimate relationships. Unfortunately, I learned the hard way that even your spouse of almost 30 years can betray you, be Abusive, cause you intentional harm and take advantage of your trusting good nature and your boundaries.

One fateful night over a pizza at the local pub, the world as I knew it came to a crashing halt. My then-husband's False Mask slipped, some of his many unethical secrets were accidentally divulged by him and the truth about his Double Life was revealed. That was my "light bulb moment." I realized from his unintentional confession that for years I had been slowly and methodically Gaslit and Narcissistically Abused. However, this time, the Abuse impacted one of our Adult Children. That was when I knew I was dealing with a monster. When he knew that I knew of his many deceits and without ever even mentioning my thoughts on wanting to leave him, the next day I was physically attacked, shoved up against the wall and verbally threatened: "Don't you dare divorce me or I will take your house, your money and your children." Unfortunately, this was one promise that he kept.

Without an exit plan, I knew at that point that there was no repairing the damage done in our relationship. This marriage was over after close to three decades. I mustered up my courage and immediately filed for divorce to escape that toxic partnership. After my Abuser was served divorce papers, he asked me if my grounds for divorce were due to "Mental Cruelty." At the time, that question seemed odd to me, however, now I understand why he asked. Abusers tell on themselves through direct comments, Projection or just a "slip of the tongue." He moved out of our marital home within a week. I chose to remain kind, hoping we could respectfully co-parent our Adult Children and remain civil in our communications.

I invited him to spend Christmas with our children in our home. I later found out he went into full gear further manipulating our family's finances (he had moved 95% of our joint and equal investments into his name only), including taking out a new department store credit card to buy Christmas presents for the kids and even me (and probably others in his Harem Supply), a maxed-out credit card bill that I would later be responsible for paying in full!

In time though, I felt that I was finally on my way to safety and freedom, however, Abusers don't let their Targets go easily or quietly and for years I continued to be obsessively smeared, stalked and silenced. In fact he continued, and still continues, to take me to court with bad faith petitions even a decade after I filed for divorce. Throughout the years of this and the hundreds of thousands of dollars spent on legal fees (I've had to have 15 lawyers!) my Abuser fears exposure and has made sure that his revealing deposition remains sealed, so that the truth of some of his unethical actions will remain hidden from the public view. His obsession with my destruction is very sick, very sad and very pathetic. He wants me silenced and I believe my life has been, and still is, in danger. The destructive behavioral patterns and legal chaos are allowed, even encouraged, by the un-justice system. The continual behavioral patterns are textbook predictable. These soul-less Abusers leave debt and destruction in their wake. The Targeted Victims are forced to engage, but throughout these ordeals, it's important to continue to go No Contact, reclaim our boundaries and get back to peace, happiness and living our best lives.

I had to learn an extremely hard lesson on finally valuing myself, my peace, my safety and my wellbeing, by waking up and connecting the dots, enough to set the ultimate Healthy Boundary in my marriage: getting divorced. Targeted Spouses are not to be blamed for the behavior of an Abuser engaged in Intimate Partner Violence, yet we must take some responsibility and ownership for allowing decades to go by where we ignored signs that the marriage was unhealthy. Part of the problem is that Abusive Spouses (men or women) will Gaslight, use Projection and slowly Isolate their partner, while they are conducting a vicious, undercover Smear Campaign so that you have limited or no support from friends, neighbors, colleagues and family. My personal situation had gone on for too many years without my awareness, that when my Gut Intuition eventually alerted me that "enough was enough" the damage was already done. I knew that I had to leave my marriage and it felt like I had to escape with my life or something detrimental would happen to me. I must still remain vigilant because there continues to be concern for my safety and well-being; Targeted spouses are at serious risk of losing their lives by their Domestic Abusers because they want you silenced and/or dead. It's unfortunately a common headline.

In addition to the shock of extreme betrayal, I lost everything that provided safety and security, including my home (which I was told was paid off for over a decade, but was actually in foreclosure), my money (cash, credit and investments) and many of my relationships (friends and neighbors who were told half-truths, most likely for years.) That was traumatic enough to jolt my reality. However, it wasn't until experiencing a parent's worst nightmare that my view of life was forever changed. I was certain that I had already endured my share of life's obstacles after escaping my Abusive Marriage, but then the unthinkable happened: I lost one of my Adult Children to extreme Parental Alienation.

The horrifying experience of unexpectedly having the loving relationship with my Adult Child abruptly severed due to vindictive Parental Alienation was the worst pain I had ever experienced. Carrying on seemed impossible because motherhood was such a huge part of how I defined myself. I was facing a crisis in midlife, just when I thought I could coast into a fabulous future. My Domestic Violence now included severe Parental Alienation — the Covert Malignant Control and Brainwashing of our children with lies, using them as aligned weapons in a war of revenge to destroy me. I was forced into a period of emotional upheaval and introspection, as it is very unnatural for a Loving Parent (mother or father) to have a child wrongly ripped away from them.

Devastated and shocked, I began questioning why bad things and injustices happen to good, upstanding people. Although my Adult Child is alive, Parental Alienation is like experiencing your child's physical death; Targeted Parents go through all of the same stages of grief. Days of no contact turn into weeks, months and in my case years. Now we're going on over a decade with this loss. It is still hard to accept that an Adult Child would estrange themselves from a Loving Parent who raised them and gave them such a wonderful life, especially after 20 years of unconditional love, care and support. Brainwashing is cult-like and the children's fear and dependency leads to "Stockholm Syndrome" where the kids align with the Abuser and "Independent Thinker Phenomenon" where the kids think the Estrangement from their Loving Parent is their idea and they are not influenced by the Alienating Parent.

Coming to terms with my new reality, I realized that people cannot control the wrongs others do to us; we can only control ourselves and how we choose to respond. An intense clarity saturated my soul. Engulfed with reassuring and peaceful feelings of pure love instead of anger, despair or vindictiveness, my heart was filled with gratitude for so many wonderful years of treasured memories and happy times. As an Erased Mom I was forced into survival mode, but despite the pain, I chose, and still continue to choose, to embrace goodness and light. Through this trauma I found writing helped me heal. It is through this healing journey that I have finally learned about setting and enforcing Healthy Boundaries.

HEALTHY BOUNDARIES AT WORK

"Individuals set boundaries to feel safe, respected and heard."
~ Pamela Cummins

Healthy Boundaries may be needed to be exercised in our work relationships. We end up spending a great deal of time with coworkers or the colleagues/superiors we are employed with at our jobs. It can be very tricky to communicate a Healthy Boundary with your colleagues and/or your boss, especially if the issue involves your being uncomfortable with a required duty or someone else's interpersonal actions.

There are many instances where it is necessary to stand up for yourself. The situations may be very minuscule or they can be significant. You may want to perform at your best, but there may be situations or people hindering you from doing that, which may warrant some clear and effective communication. Because you are in an environment with varying personality types, you must also take into consideration and be sensitive to the fact that everyone has different ways of interacting and communicating.

At work, you may experience constant interruptions where a coworker is monopolizing your time with their issues. You may be asked to work overtime or put in extra hours without compensation. Your physical space may be violated when someone gets too friendly and wants to hug or connect deeper, when you don't; that's when you must perfect the art of the professional handshake and set some Healthy Boundaries.

There also may be competition in the workplace. If a colleague wants to get ahead and is ruthless, they may sabotage you, your work or your relationships just to give themselves the upper hand. People will go to great lengths so you don't get recognized or are offered that well-deserved promotion, when they are also in line for the same. They may take credit for a project that you did. They may move your stuff around or even steal important documents. They may just simply Gaslight you to make you question your abilities or make you believe that you are not as capable as you really are. Smear Campaigns based on outright lies or believable half-truths happen in jobs as well, where your good name can be tarnished with a False Narrative. There is no limit to what some people are capable of doing. The workplace can be very positive, but it can also be a toxic place where some believe they have the right to exercise Abusive power and control.

It has been widely known that there are some bosses that use their power and positions to get those working below them to deviate from their assigned and hired roles. It can be very easy to be taken advantage of by someone who lacks integrity and is very demanding and self-serving. Also, Sexual Harassment is a real phenomenon. So many workers are afraid to speak up because they don't want to lose their job and get fired. Sometimes, there can be backlash if you do stand up for yourself and bring their behavior into question. Whistleblowers are often silenced. A toxic workplace can be an extremely challenging environment where it may be necessary to set Healthy Boundaries.

In the workplace, take time to understand each other's roles and the expectations required to fulfill your duties and responsibilities. You can learn how to say "no" in a polite, yet assertive way. It is important to be careful when the lines at work get blurred. Remain professional at all times. In some instances, the only realistic solution is to quit and find another job. When Healthy Boundaries are set and enforced in our work environments, team members feel more comfortable and valued, which has positive implications on the production of the organization as a whole.

HEALTHY BOUNDARIES
WITH FRIENDS

Those who get angry when you set a boundary
are the ones you need to set boundaries for."
~ J. S. Wolfe

Healthy Boundaries are not only important for our romantic or work relationships, they can be needed with our friendships as well. My lightbulb moment happened during a phone conversation with a lifelong, childhood "best friend" where we were briefly discussing some political news headline. I had very respectfully and in a non-confrontational way, shared that I disagreed with her viewpoint, and looked at the situation differently. I had no idea that voicing my own, different views would turn out to actually be me indirectly setting a relatively simple Healthy Boundary at that given time. I was certainly not prepared for her subsequent comments and was shocked because her reaction was totally unexpected. Even though we were the very best of friends for half of a century, into midlife, and I thought our relationship was solid, she didn't make any effort to acknowledge my feelings or that we could "agree to disagree." This time, I took notice.

She did not take this situation of our differing opinions as an opportunity to reassure me, understand my perspective or acknowledge her acceptance of our opposite viewpoints in order to keep our lifelong friendship moving forward. Her reaction to my voicing my own perspective, which resulted in my setting a very simple Healthy Boundary, really told me everything I needed to know. It was then that I had to take a deep look at a number of situations of her reactions and interactions over the span of this friendship.

I realized that there was a lifelong pattern in our relationship where this childhood friend seemed to know best and be the authority on all things. In fact, at one point she said to me, "I know you, your husband, your children, your mom and dad and your entire family better than you know them." At the time of her saying this comment and reflecting back on the many other times I felt scolded by her, I did feel uncomfortable and thought that she was crossing a line, yet I never was one to confront, so I didn't. Plus, Abusive Others are skilled at using Intermittent Reinforcement to keep you hooked to go along, often for years and years. She would intersperse heartwarming moments and what appeared to be sincere and caring comments sporadically to keep me in check, hooked and Trauma Bonded. My silence and allowing her to make statements like this, along with my foundational traumas mixed with the feeling that we had so much soul-sister history together contributed to this pattern continuing for years. I am at fault at allowing this.

In addition to my doubting myself due to experiencing years of Gaslighting from a number of people on a number of fronts, I never looked at myself as a "know it all" and was always open to other's perspectives on most everything. I was not judgmental and accepted others and their differences. In some ways I acted like a neutral peace keeper, because I never challenged other's opinions. In assuming this role, however, I also never stood up for myself and never put up Healthy Boundaries. The various issues and situations never seemed to warrant a major reaction from me. This was yet another life lesson that I needed to finally learn. Unfortunately, I'm just learning this late in my life.

This "best friend" always seemed to me to be jealous of the free spirit, worldly experiences and inner drive I had throughout our childhood, as her life was more stifled and controlled than mine. I just chalked it up to the expression that "opposites attract." We did share many great times and laughs together. We were raised in households that were very different; my parents were more liberal in their parenting style, so I was left on my own a lot to navigate life. Back then I didn't feel neglected or abandoned, although looking back, when I think of my dad's drinking and affairs, my mom's diagnosis of "mental illness," my being hungry when the cupboards were bare or the time I rode my bike several miles to the hospital because I needed stitches, I wonder. Either way, despite surviving my parents' contentious divorce, I am appreciative to them for all they did, the experiences they gave me, and the independence, creativity and love of learning they instilled in me, so I must have had more care than I realized to make it into adulthood. However, I now must acknowledge the negatives and inconsistencies in my upbringing. I was then and am now still a Survivor.

This "best friend" had a more structured, traditional family unit with strict rules and behavioral expectations. Unlike me, she had to contend with a great deal of guilt and authoritarian "dos and don'ts." Her mom would ring a dinner bell that could be heard throughout the neighborhood every evening at the same time. I remember seeing the fear in my friend's eyes and the physical shaking of her body when that daily dinner bell rang, as she had to immediately stop playing and run home for dinner. Even though I was adventurous and followed my dreams with no hesitation, I now believe that I was always subconsciously seeking the structure and stability that was lacking in my family unit. Throughout our childhood and our different upbringings, I still believed that this "best friend" was my forever-rock, that we would always have each other and that we would grow old together. I can see now that her scolding and domineering actions towards me over the years were really a result of her enduring that same treatment growing up.

Reflecting back on our relationship, it was clear that we did not have the same values on a number of fairly significant things. We both enjoyed getting together drinking and dancing with others at parties, yet when she experimented with and later continued to use harder, more dangerous substances, I wanted nothing to do with that. We still remained friends even though our views and experiences regarding drug use were different. She never pressured me and I never confronted her. Back then, we could agree to disagree, even if it was just by our actions.

She had several abortions. I never challenged her decisions because they were her personal decisions and not mine to chime in on. For as long as I can remember I wanted to be a mother more than anything in my life and knew that whether I was married or not and I found myself pregnant, I would never, ever abort a baby. I personally value all life and believe that life begins at conception. Our moral compass and ethical leanings were different and she obviously didn't look at this the same way I did. Back then, we could agree to disagree, even on such serious issues, yet we could still remain friends.

We both had serious boyfriends over the years and eventually married, yet she continued to engage in numerous extramarital affairs, once even with a married man who had a young family. I valued fidelity and would never even think of cheating on my then-husband, even though I later learned of his extramarital affairs and that our marriage vows were not sacred to him. My "best friend" and I both seemed to accept and understand each other for who we were and never put each other down or challenged the issues or differences in values. Back then, we could agree to disagree, even over the issue of fidelity, lying and cheating.

Although she was dishonest with and would badmouth others with her strong opinions over the many years, I never once though she would lie to or backstab me, her "best friend." The reality was that I was pretty naive and turned a blind eye where I should have been more discerning and aware. In fact, looking back, this "best friend" with her persistent Gaslighting was the driving force for my basically dropping a close teacher friend. It's too late for me to rectify that situation, but I surely can learn from it. These Narcissists want you isolated so that you become dependent on only them.

At one point out of the blue my "best friend" called me "condescending," which was shocking and a complete and obvious Projection, as I was never condescending. Our entire lives she was always very dismissive and condescending to me, although I never stood up for myself and confronted her about how I felt. Again, I had a lot to learn about valuing myself enough to set Healthy Boundaries. She was skilled at Gaslighting me to believe I was not smart enough to take care of basic tasks, even though I had many more years of formal schooling than she had and was a capable, accomplished and successful individual. My low self-worth allowed such damaging patterns to play out into adulthood.

As we got older, this lifelong, "best friend" seemed to continue to covet my life in a few more ways. I had a small group of high school friends that I had recently reconnected with after a 40ᵗʰ class reunion. These friends were in the same extracurricular activities as me and we had a great and fun connection in high school and were on our way to rekindling our relationships. On one of our gatherings together I invited this lifelong, childhood "best friend" to join us for dinner. Even though she knew of my group of friends because we were all in the same graduating class, my "best friend" never had a relationship with them during or after high school, even though they all lived close to one another. We all hit it off and got together several times. Then things changed.

I had no idea that she was slowly monopolizing the relationships with my high school classmates. They now became much closer with her than me, so much so, that after I stepped away and went No Contact from my "best friend," my high school friends stopped calling. Then weeks later, one of them contacted me through an impersonal group text. I knew right away that it was not sincere and was a Flying Monkey effort on behalf of my "best friend." When that attempt was unsuccessful because I did not return the communication, this entire group of friends stopped contacting me altogether. I can't even imagine the lies she told them about me, or that they would even believe them. Luckily I don't care. This really didn't bother me, but as the years went on, I did take notice of this situation because it was one of many instances where I could see a pattern of her stepping into relationships that were once mine.

Another friend scenario involved a neighbor who I was very close with for decades. Our children were of similar ages and we raised our families in the same cul-de-sac and shared many years of support, heartfelt conversations and good times together. When I eventually chose to file for divorce, I was shocked to learn that our home was not paid off as I was assured for the past ten years. My home was actually in foreclosure! Turns out that I would have to move from our beautiful neighborhood. It was around that same time that I began to notice that all of my neighbors, who I was previously friendly with, stopped talking to me, including this close neighbor. This neighbor, however, connected with my "best friend."

I later learned about how Narcissistic ex-spouses conduct a Smear Campaign that disparages the Targeted Spouse, getting everyone and anyone to side with them, by spreading a False Narrative of outright lies and believable half-truths. With a surprise turn of events, afterwards, my lifelong "best friend" also engaged in a Smear Campaign and became very close with my neighbor. I knew that they had met casually here or there, but it was like she was, yet again, stepping into another relationship that I had built over the many years. I knew it was a bit odd, but I just moved on and let the entire situation slip away, as I was dealing with so many other things at the time. They both really showed their True Colors.

The final boundary this lifelong, "best friend" crossed, well, at least the big one that I was aware of, hit very close to my heartstrings as a Loving Mom. I've come to learn that Narcissistic People like this habitually lie, cheat and steal and secrets can be kept for a lifetime; many even have physical or emotional affairs with their best friend's spouse without them ever finding out. This next particularly shocking betrayal involved my beautiful, Alienated Adult Child, and strangely, our family's pet cat.

Turns out, a big part of the Domestic Violence I endured as a result of being married to someone with traits similar to that of a Covert Malignant Narcissist, is that I experienced (and continue to experience a decade after filing for divorce) extreme Parental Alienation of one of our two Adult Children, which happened shortly after I escaped my 27-year marriage. It was when I was retiring after 35 years from my rewarding and successful teaching career and moving over 2,000 miles away from the Chicago Suburbs to the Caribbean with my life partner who is deathly allergic to cats, that this "best friend" offered to help me find my cat a new, loving home. I gladly gave her money without knowing that she was actually extorting me for hundreds of dollars without providing much information. I eventually saw the social media posts where she secretly enlisted my Adult Child in the adoption efforts and I learned of what really happened to my furry feline. This was such a painful time for me, as I loved and adored my Alienated Child so much, and also loved our family's pet cat. This "best friend" betrayed me and was engaging in ongoing communication with my child without telling me, knowing how shocked and heartbroken I was to be experiencing Parental Alienation. Such deliberate deceit!

The losses I had endured were devastatingly mind-boggling. I learned years after the Alienation, where I lost all contact with this Adult Child, that my "best friend" was over- stepping into my maternal role and communicating with my child on a regular basis, without ever telling me. All the years of missed milestones and holidays where I was heartbroken, my friend never once told me where my child lived or how they were. Unbelievable deception! Lying by omission! Betrayal at the deepest level! In fact, there were a number of times I stopped by my friend's home because I was in her area for the day, yet each time she came to the door saying she was busy and I couldn't come in, not even for a few moments. It sure seemed like she was hiding something (or someone) from me, yet I just let this go without question. I allowed and accepted this deception.

Because my "best friend" does not have or ever wanted children, I believe she has no real clue about the deep feelings and bonds shared between mother and child, especially when coping with Alienation and your Adult Child not being in your life. Experts and researchers state that Parental Alienation is the most devastating form of Intimate Partner Violence by an ex-spouse or others, with the grieving compared to a Loving Parent experiencing the physical death of losing your child. I went through all the stages of grief.

With regards to my cat, I thought it very odd, yet didn't question it when my "best friend" refused to tell me who adopted my cat, even though she insisted that I continue to pay her unusually large sums of money for its care, indefinitely. She would not share any details or receipts with me. I went along with this, still believing that this "best friend" was looking out for me and would never hurt me, let alone extort money from me or not share information about my Alienated Child. Maybe my cat's life journey involved being the "cat"alyst to my becoming aware of the "True Deceit False Love" from this "best friend."

This friend was secretly taking over my role as mother, confidant and sympathizer, and contributed significantly to the Alienation of my Adult Child. In a very stealth manner, she inserted herself "in loco parentis" into my family and caused disruption and continued heartache with her misguided and damaging influence. I was wronged on so many levels. My blind faith, foundational patterns, trust in the goodness of others and my very, very weak boundaries kept me from seeing the truth of the Best Friend Betrayal that I was experiencing, and had experienced for many years. I take responsibility for allowing this to continue, but shame on her for what she did. After all this reflection, I finally realized that the way I felt around her, as well as our extreme differences in values, was something that I could no longer comfortably live with. It was definitely time to set boundaries.

As painful as it was, I chose to quietly step away from this "best friend." In doing so, I had to, in a sense, mourn the loss of this lifelong relationship. In some ways this decision was harder than my choice to divorce my Abusive Husband after 27 years of marriage. I had known her my entire life! After I decided to go No Contact without any effort from her to communicate, I became acutely aware that she embarked on a devastating Smear Campaign, spreading a False Narrative to people I was close to, including my childhood, high school and adult friends, neighbors and immediate family members. All of a sudden my positive qualities became negative. Well, it most likely wasn't all of a sudden. People who do this, patiently and with great calculation, spend years setting the stage to discredit and sabotage you. This relationship was an example of "True Deceit and False Love" and Best Friend Betrayal.

I didn't realize that for over 50 years I was Trauma-Bonded with this "best friend," and I had to once again learn a lot about Gaslighting and Projection. After much self-reflection and analyzing the patterns that I allowed in this relationship, I am proud of myself that I chose to go No Contact. No discussion. No explanation. I just stopped communicating and blocked her number and email. I never heard from her again. If a friend was truly a friend, they would find some way to reach out to talk things over and make efforts to communicate and repair the issue. Nothing. Wow! That was a reality check for me. At least I really knew where I stood and was confident in my assessment of the relationship. Actually, it's now a relief as I have stopped ruminating on her and how I felt all these years.

As a result of my courageous decision and actions to let go of this unhealthy relationship, I feel stronger and more aware. Knowledge is power. I have

DR. MARNI HILL FODERARO

accepted the outcome. I have not looked back negatively on the many years of our friendship, as I now realize that this was yet another big life lesson that I needed to learn. I had to realize that the people she poisoned against me, who never once contacted me to get my take on the situation, were really not true friends and people who don't deserve to be in my life anyway.

I needed to understand Best Friend Betrayal and Trauma Bonding and my role in this over 50-year friendship and make necessary changes to my own thoughts and behavior so that my future relationships would be more balanced and healthy. I had to understand rejection, abandonment, trust, belonging and my own issues with worthiness and confidence. I have accepted this situation, learned from it and have moved on. Actually, through this and other experiences, I have found that when loving, empathetic people release toxic or psychologically Abusive people from our life, it opens the door and allows room to welcome others in who share our same values and integrity.

HEALTHY BOUNDARIES
WITH FAMILY

*"Families living in dysfunction seldom have healthy
boundaries. Dysfunctional families have trouble
knowing where they stop and others begin."*
~ David W. Earle

Setting Healthy Boundaries may also be needed with some of our family
members. We have all heard the sayings that "blood is thicker than
water" or "you can choose your friends, but you can't choose your family."
There are certain societal expectations that frown upon setting Healthy
Boundaries with family members and there is less public conversation
and professional support for breaking free from family, even if there is
toxic Abuse within the family system. It is very common for there to be
disagreements, differences in opinions and conflicts on a wide array of issues
between various members in a family, whether they are within the small
immediate family unit or with extended family relatives. These issues are
clouded by the familial hierarchy, expectations and roles. Often there are
power and control issues, especially from those who hold the purse strings
or dole out the discipline. Many innocent people have been emotionally,

physically and financially abused by members of their own family who they trusted or were dependent on. Many Victims have permanent scars as a result of incest and sexual Abuse by a parent or extended family member. It is shocking and hard to comprehend or accept, but some parents later find out after divorcing that their own, now Adult Children were sexually Abused by their ex-spouse.

There are also many cases of Domestic Violence and Parental Alienation that negatively impact the relationships within families. Many well-meaning, Loving Parents struggle with setting Healthy Boundaries with their own Adult Children, where the lines are blurred between helping their child and enabling unhealthy behaviors, especially when drug addiction is involved. Adult children can be Narcissistic, dishonest and manipulative, and that is very hard for a parent to see or accept that their own flesh and blood can be capable of lying, cheating and stealing. It's hard to accept that their Adult Child's personality and behaviors may be completely different than the person they raised and once knew.

Sibling Rivalry is all-too-common in families, however Alienating Parents take this to another level by using the Divide and Conquer method to purposely cause conflict between and isolate brothers and sisters from each other, often times because that Abusing Parent has secrets to hide and don't want their kids to compare notes to question, discover and possibly expose the truth. These Abusers have no problems going to great lengths to silence the truth.

It's important to remember that setting Healthy Boundaries and even stepping away from familial relationships can very much be an act of love and care. I know this sounds conflicting, but just because we eventually came to a crossroads where we chose to set limits on what we will and won't tolerate, it doesn't mean we don't love our family members deeply. Sometimes we find the need to eventually reevaluate our family relationships, and we need to give ourselves permission to honor our own feelings and needs to live in peace with less turmoil. Sometimes we must go No Contact as the only means to setting Healthy Boundaries with family members.

Experiencing my own high-conflict divorce after close to three decades, extreme Parental Alienation and the loss of friendships, including a best, lifelong friend, I really needed to look inward to my foundational patterns within my family of origin. After experiencing the Gaslighting, Projection and Betrayal that comes with enduring Domestic Violence, Narcissistic Abuse and Parental Alienation and then taking ownership and responsibility for my role in the unhealthy, unbalanced family dynamics, I did a deep dive into the literature and research on understanding Intergenerational Family Trauma to move in a positive direction on my healing journey.

Addressing the issues with my family of origin was long overdue. After going though the fallout of my marriage and realizing that I completely misjudged the person who I was married to, experiencing losing most everything and everyone that provided me with a sense of security, and ultimately losing my Adult Children to Parental Alienation, losing my home, money and assets and discovering that I lost my friends, neighbors, coworkers, even people I knew from church or served with as a Girl Scout Leader, all from an aggressive and damaging Smear Campaign, it was necessary for me to take a closer look at my foundational patterns, immediate family and my role in this situation.

I desperately wanted to hold on to my immediate family, especially during these challenging times when I learned that so many other relationships in my life were not as healthy as I once believed. We are conditioned by society to believe that our flesh and blood is supposed to love us unconditionally and be there for us at all times. Such expectations often go unfulfilled. I forced myself to engage in a great deal of reflection and analysis of the relationship dynamics of my immediate family: my parents, stepparent, and siblings. I also really needed to take a long hard look at my role in these relationships, and how our interactions evolved over our lifetimes. I realize that even though we are from the same family, our memories of our experiences or views of our experiences can be quite different. It's hard to realize and acknowledge that there is dysfunction and unhealthy interactions within our own families.

Over the many years, I spent a great deal of time, energy and money reaching out to show my sincere love to my family, often to the point of over-giving with thoughtful, personal and generous gifts; this applied to extended family as well. These efforts were not always well-received or even acknowledged, however in my opinion, they were certainly done in a thoughtful spirit and were well-intentioned. I gave freely with no expectations or strings attached. I did eventually notice certain behavioral patterns after researching and learning about toxic and/or Abusive relationships. I paid attention when some common Gaslighting phrases were said to me from my father, like: "Oh, c'mon, you're overreacting," "Don't be so sensitive," "I have in effect told you that I was mistaken," "Put it behind you," "You heard me wrong," and "You surely can't blame me for having affairs as your mother was so sick." It was tough for me to accept, but my interest in their lives, well-being and activities weren't reciprocated. Very little was asked about how I was doing and certainly no recognition was given to me for most of my major life accomplishments that I had achieved. At the time I didn't make a big deal of this as I was conditioned over the years to not need attention and didn't seek out validation. Now I was really seeing things for what they were; I was "seeing the forest through the trees."

Finally, through this self-reflection and research, I was gaining the inner strength that I was lacking for most of my life. Even though it was very sad and painful for me to make this decision, I found that even though I loved my family dearly, it was the best for my own well-being and happiness to put up Healthy Boundaries and go No Contact with two family members and their spouses. Their reactions, but more significantly, their lack of reactions, were very telling. There were no sincere efforts to reach out and communicate to find some common understanding, let alone any acknowledgement of my feelings or an apology. Instead, there was basically very little response, except for a random and selfish, guilt-ridden email where the blame, shame and accusations were placed solely on me. This confirmed for me that I was justified in setting Healthy Boundaries and breaking off communications with these family members. I didn't see these relationships improving. It hurts and is still painful, but I am glad that I eventually learned to value myself and my feelings. Setting Healthy Boundaries is not an easy task.

We are molded, in part, by our foundational experiences and relationships. It is within our family that we learn about love and we are witness to how that is expressed. In dysfunctional families, which includes many of us, we do not always experience positive role models. We go along life burying the negative, while we forge ahead in our efforts to create a positive life for ourselves. We often take our family for granted and assume that they love us unconditionally and would never harm us. The reality is that there is much baggage and bad behavior in families. There are many resentments, which I believe are really unfulfilled expectations.

I have always loved my family with all my heart. I especially love the two family members and their spouses with whom I eventually needed to step away from, for my own peace and well-being. The playbooks of Narcissistic Abusers are so similar. In fact, some of the comments told to me by both were classic and common statements of Gaslighting, Blame Shifting and Projection. Even the Flying Monkey efforts and Guilt Tripping were easy to spot, now that I've learned the common and general tactics used. I was able to connect the dots to the patterns from my childhood to adulthood, and see things as they really were: dismissive and condescending. More importantly, I analyzed how I felt before, during and after each interaction. I didn't like how I felt and enough was enough. But it was more than that, I had to accept that I was not truly valued as I believe I should be. I also had to look within at my desperate efforts over many decades to show love my love to them. Even though I looked at my efforts as compassionate, caring and thoughtful, they were not always received that way. The goalposts were constantly moved. Now I understand more. I still love my family and always will, but after everything I've been through, I need to love myself first and foremost. It's because of this that I had to put up and will continue to enforce Healthy Boundaries within my family.

WE ARE STRONGER
THAN WE BELIEVE

"Create boundaries. Honor your limits. Say no.
Take a break. Let go. Stay grounded.
Nurture your body. Love your vulnerability.
And if all else fails, breathe deeply."
~ Aletheia Luna

It would be ideal in all of our relationships if we could identify and communicate the boundary that has been crossed and what consequences would happen to the relationship if the person we are experiencing this with continues their behavior. It would be ideal if they would hear us, feel bad or remorseful and wanted to make the changes necessary to repair the discord. It would be ideal if their reaction was to let us know that they value us enough to be more sensitive to our feelings. It would be ideal if they didn't react negatively to us expressing the need to set a Healthy Boundary. The reality, however, is that if we are at this point, there are very few people who would react in this ideal way. If we are at this point, we must realize the great possibility that setting a Healthy Boundary could result in the end of the relationship, especially if the person is toxic or psychologically Abusive.

We do, however, need to give ourselves credit for finally realizing that we have the ability to determine what we will and should tolerate in our relationships. We can't beat ourselves up for not knowing what we didn't know before we knew it. It's all part of the journey of the life lessons that we must learn as we navigate our time on this earth. Relational patterns can be leftover baggage from past experiences that molded us into who we are and what we will accept. Patterns are learned and are often passed down from generation to generation. If we begin to feel that we are disrespected or dismissed, we need to muster up the courage to value ourselves enough to break the patterns that we have actually allowed. The additional challenge is to accept the outcome. Be prepared for the harsh reality that we may learn the true nature of others and that our relationship was not what we thought, wanted or believed.

There is a power in honest dialogue and a strength in sharing our experiences, because when we are heard, we are also seen and validated. It takes a great deal of courage to embrace our vulnerabilities and set Healthy Boundaries. You can heal and triumph over challenges and the malevolent actions, habits and Abuse of others. Awareness is the first step. We need to follow our Gut Intuition when our lightbulb is finally illuminated to show us that a change in some of our relationships is warranted. This only happens when we are at a stage where we get out of the FOG (Fear, Obligation and Guilt) and denial. Not only is it painful to realize that there are serious imbalances and discord with people we love, such as parents, siblings and best friends, there are a wide array of emotions that surface when we must face the fact that our own foundational patterns, beliefs and actions actually contributed significantly to this unhealthy relationship dynamic continuing and gaining strength as the years go on. Cut yourself some slack so you can make the necessary changes now to prevent from being further used and Abused. Loving yourself more than pleasing others is a concept that was most likely a long time in coming, but the time is now to put up and enforce Healthy Boundaries.

We deserve to be in relationships based on mutual respect. In order to have positive relationships moving forward, we must acknowledge how we feel and whether or not those in our circle act in ways that reinforce we are valued. We have every right to honor ourselves when it comes to who we let and keep in our lives by putting up Healthy Boundaries. We cannot control the actions of others, but we can control ourselves and how we respond. Healthy Boundaries are opportunities to love ourselves unconditionally and have our own backs. Our awareness is then heightened and we become more open to the signs and synchronicities on our Spiritual Journey. Healthy Boundaries are about teaching others who we are and learning about who others are. We have the duty to ourselves to stay true to our integrity and values to put up and enforce Healthy Boundaries. We are stronger than we believe.

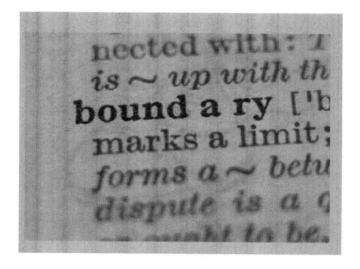

"*The hardest part about setting boundaries with people, no matter who they are, is not feeling confident in our authority to do so. As long as you realize that setting boundaries is necessary for healthy relationships, you will feel better defining and keeping them.*"
~ Tamera Mowry-Housley

"NO is a complete sentence."
~Anne Lamott

Check out the other books in the
TRUE DECEIT FALSE LOVE series!

Printed in the United States
by Baker & Taylor Publisher Services